PRESTON TO LANCASTER

West Coast Main Line

Roy Davies

MP Middleton Press

Front cover: BR Class 40s head a Scottish double. No. 40136 (left) has just taken over 1M84 09.13 Edinburgh - Blackpool North alongside sister loco no. 40036 (right) on the 1M21 08.30 Glasgow Central - Blackpool North on a wet Saturday, 22nd August 1981. These locomotives would probably have taken over from electric traction for the final part of the journey to the coast. (Peter Smith)

Back cover map: Railway Clearing House map, dated 1947. The route of the album is shown with a dotted line.

Back cover photo: On 8th June 2021 Colas Rail Class 37 No. 37254 Cardiff Canton *hauls the Plain Line Pattern Recognition (PLPR) test train with Class 37 No. 37175 tailing over the Condor viaduct at Galgate. (Will Smith)*

ACKNOWLEDGEMENTS

I am very grateful for the assistance received from Ron Herbert, Preston Digital Archive, Lens of Sutton Association (LOSA), LNWR Association, RailScot, Dave Stubbins & Cumbria Railway Association, Jan Ford, K.Nuttal, and T.Rawlings (deceased).

I am also thankful for the assistance received from many of those mentioned in the credits, as well as from G. Croughton, G. Gartside, C.M. Howard, N. Langridge, B. Read, D. and Dr S. Salter, P.D.Shannon and M. Stewart.

Published September 2022

ISBN 978 1 910356 74 6

© *Middleton Press Ltd, 2022*

Cover design and Photo Editor Deborah Esher
Production Editor Cassandra Morgan

Published by
    Middleton Press Ltd
    Camelsdale Road
    Haslemere
    Surrey
    GU27 3RJ
Tel: 01730 813169
Email: info@middletonpress.co.uk
www.middletonpress.co.uk

Printed and bound by CPI Group (UK) Ltd, Croydon, CR0 4YY

Abbreviations:

Advanced Passenger Train (APT)
Bolton and Preston Railway (B&PR)
Direct Rail Services (DRS)
English Welsh & Scottish (EWS)
Garstang & Knott End Railway (GKER)
Grand Junction Railway (GJR)
Great British Railways (GBR)
Lancaster and Carlisle Railway (L&CR)
Lancaster and Preston Junction Railway (L&PJR)
Lancashire and Yorkshire Railway (L&Y)
London and Birmingham Railway (L&BR)
London Midland and Scottish Railway (LMS)
London Midland Region (LMR)
London and North Western Railway (LNWR)
North Union Railway (NUR)
Train Operating Companies (TOCs)
TransPennine Express (TPE)
Virgin Trains (VT)
West Lancashire Railway (WLR)

CONTENTS

I. The Railway Clearing House map of 1947 has the route of this album in dark grey.

GEOGRAPHICAL SETTING

The line runs almost due north until the outskirts of Lancaster where the line curves to the west and then north again as it approaches Lancaster Station. The whole route is virtually parallel to the M6 motorway to the east and the A6 to the west until Galgate, where it crosses the trunk road on the Skew Bridge, and runs into Lancaster. After a gentle climb out of Preston the line is relatively level throughout until it reaches the former Lancaster Old Junction where it falls steeply on the 1 in 98 gradient towards the approach into Lancaster. The Lancaster Canal runs to the west of the railway and occasionally can be seen from the line and is eventually crossed just south of Lancaster station. The terrain is undulating as the Bowling Fells level out to the west and this is negotiated by way of cuttings and embankments most notably the Condor viaduct at Galgate that crosses the river of that name. The only other significant structure on the route is the bridge crossing the River Wyre just north of Scorton.

In general, maps are based on the 25ins to the mile Ordnance Survey editions with north at the top. Other scales and maps have been used where appropriate and indicated accordingly.

HISTORICAL BACKGROUND

Take the 21 mile (34km) trip from Preston to Lancaster today and you will experience a smooth journey taking under 20 minutes. Back in the 1840s it was a very bumpy ride indeed. This was due to a multitude of problems, such as: incompetent management; poor engineering and construction; safety concerns; lack of motive power and rolling stock; underfunding and railway company rivalry. Things did not really settle until the Lancaster and Carlisle Railway (L&CR) took control of the line in 1848.

Whereas the nascent East Coast Main Line was conceived early on as a trunk route and constructed in the 1840s by the three companies already operating between London and Edinburgh, later to amalgamate to form the London and North Eastern Railway, construction of the West Coast Main Line was very much piecemeal by comparison as exemplified by the section from Preston to Lancaster, which, it could be argued, was the final link in the important railway corridor that we know today.

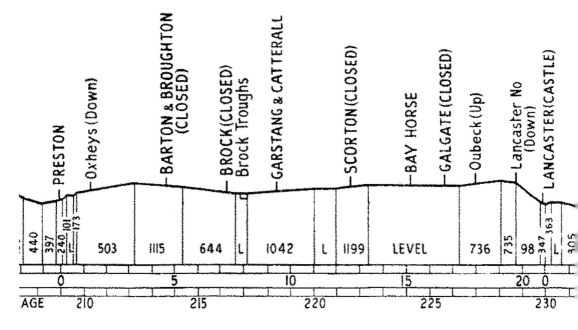

The railway first came to Preston courtesy of the North Union Railway (NUR) in October 1838; the NUR came into being in 1834 by way of the first amalgamation of two railway companies in the UK, namely: the Wigan Branch Railway and the Preston and Wigan Railway. The L&CR along with its counterpart, the Caledonian Railway, had already made plans to link Lancaster with Scotland and it wasn't long before the residents and particularly the merchants of Lancaster were pushing for a line linking the City of Lancaster with Preston and on 5th May 1837 the Lancaster and Preston Junction Railway (L&PJR) was authorised by Parliament. Construction started soon after with Joseph Locke appointed Engineer.

The line was opened on 25th June 1840 and the Lancaster terminus of the L&PJR was located just south of the Lancaster Canal on South Road. Initially the line terminated in Preston just to the north of Fishergate at Dock Street adjacent to the Lancaster Canal basin. There were eight intermediate stations in all on the route, some very short lived, as well as five branch lines along the route. These subsidiary lines will be covered in Middleton Press album, *Branch Lines Around Preston and Lancaster*.

The L&PJR was in a chaotic situation soon after its opening; it did not have a legally constituted board of directors and management was poor. By 1842 the L&PJR was suffering losses as business had not developed as anticipated due mainly to competition from the Lancaster Canal Company that had been in operation since 1833; it was weakened also by the ongoing conflict with the NUR for rights at Preston. Because of its precarious financial situation, the L&PJR sought to lease the line; both the Manchester, Bolton and Bury Railway and the NUR turned it down but on 1st September 1842 an agreement was reached with the Canal Company to lease the line for 21 years at a charge of £30,000 pa.

The aforementioned conflict with the NUR turned on two main issues: (1) the L&PJR amenities at Preston and (2) locomotive operating arrangements.

(1) Before the L&PJR line was completed the NUR agreed to extend northwards by tunnelling under Fishergate and building a joint station at Dock Street. The L&PJR agreed to pay a contribution of £1,500 towards the cost of the extension, end-on junction, the platform and running powers to the NUR's Butler Street station. It then transpired that the L&PJR did not have free use of the Dock Street facilities or running powers to Butler Street. Having made the capital contribution, the L&PJR was not minded to pay tolls for using the amenities.

(2) Late in the day the L&PJR agreed a locomotive operating arrangement with the NUR but there was friction; first the NUR found that the track was substandard claiming that its locomotives were being damaged and second that the L&PJR did not fulfil its side of the bargain and so the NUR withdrew from the arrangement. In early 1841, Lancashire born John Hargreaves, an established freight carrier, railway entrepreneur and local man, took over working freight traffic on the line as well as operating the L&PJR locomotives that were provided by the Manchester, Bolton and Bury Railway.

The conflict between the NUR and L&PJR was heightened when the latter formed an alliance with the Bolton and Preston Railway (B&PR), which the NUR considered an adversary. The B&PR intended to utilise the Lancaster Canal Tramway, which connected the two portions of the Lancaster Canal and crossing the Ribble Valley in the process, and have its own station at Preston. Accordingly, it reserved a site north of Fishergate on land occupied by Maxwell House by which the station was sometimes known and not far from the Dock Street station. 'Maxwell House' station opened on 1st January 1842 and the L&PJR used it from that date. The NUR responded by charging through passengers the princely sum of 6d for the journey from Dock Street to its Butler Street station. As a consequence, some walked the 200 yards (183m) from one station to the other but at the risk of missing their onward connection.

The NUR and B&PR were basically in competition on their respective Manchester to Preston routes and undercut each other's fares but the NUR had the advantage of charging the B&PR high tolls for its running powers over the Euxton to Preston section of the route. Financially weakened by this rivalry the B&PR was first amalgamated in 1843 then acquired by the NUR on 1st January 1844 along with ownership of Maxwell House station, which the L&PJR was then barred from using. For a while passengers had to detrain on the trackside until 12th February 1844 when the NUR and L&PJR agreed that regular trains could use the Butler Street station subject to a rental agreement between the NUR and the Canal Company effective 13th February 1844. Maxwell House was retained for a few months thereafter for excursion traffic.

The 22nd September 1846 saw the public opening of the L&CR line from Kendal Junction (changed to Oxenholme in 1860) to Lancaster with Lancaster Castle station serving as its southern terminus. As the line north from Kendal Junction to Carlisle was under construction, the Caledonian Railway was pressing on with the line north to central Scotland. The directors of the L&CR were anxious to run through to Preston and link up with the network beyond and the route through to London and so constructed a link to the L&PJR line; there is no clear evidence but it is most likely the L&CR line was extended southwards to join the L&PJR at what later became Lancaster Old Junction.

While the L&PJR and NUR were having their spat over access etc at Preston, the L&CR and L&PJR were also in dispute regarding running rights over the line to Preston. Mention has already been made of the lack of stewardship of the L&PJR, which made it nigh on impossible for the L&CR to strike a deal with the company; so much so that the L&CR even considered seeking powers to build its own independent line to Preston. The dispute turned mainly on the higher-than-average tolls the L&PJR was charging and, as a consequence of the ensuing impasse, the L&CR gave notice that it intended to use the L&PJR line and pay no tolls; instead, the L&CR would keep a record of journeys made and pay any dues as decided by a court of law or through arbitration. This arrangement obviated the need for an alternative route to Preston and in 1848 an agreement was reached whereby the L&CR took over management and operation of the L&PJR with the latter coming to an end in all but name. In addition, the L&PJR Lancaster terminus was closed to passengers on 1st August 1849, the date when the line was leased to the L&CR, and services transferred to the more centrally located Lancaster Castle station. The fate of the L&PJR was finally sealed on 13th August 1859 when it was amalgamated with the L&CR.

By 1838 Preston was linked to London via the NUR, the Grand Junction Railway (GJR) and the London and Birmingham Railway (L&BR). Next came absorption of various railway companies by the London and North Western Railway (LNWR), which was incorporated on 16th July 1846. In the same year the LNWR sought to acquire both the L&BR and GJR but the GJR was already in discussion to merge with the Manchester and Leeds Railway along with many other concerns to become the Lancashire and Yorkshire Railway (L&Y) in 1847. Subsequently the LNWR and L&Y agreed to jointly lease the NUR; this arrangement continued until 26th July 1889 when it (NUR) was acquired jointly by the two companies. With the amalgamation of the L&PJR and the L&CR in 1859, this joint enterprise was leased to the LNWR giving it a direct route from London to Carlisle.

Prior to the implementation of the Railways Act of 1921, the L&Y merged with the LNWR on 1st January 1922 and exactly a year later the London Midland and Scottish Railway (LMS) was incorporated under the Act of 1921. The main companies that merged into the LMS included the combined LNWR and L&Y, the Midland Railway and the Caledonian Railway. This meant that Preston and Lancaster became important stopping points on the now seamless WCML.

Next came the Transport Act 1947 that brought about the nationalisation of British Railways (BR) and saw services at Preston, Lancaster and the remaining intermediate stations fall under the London Midland Region (LMR). In the 1950s BR embarked on a modernisation programme that was to include diesels replacing steam locomotives, and a continuation of the electrification of the network, resignalling and track renewals, improved coaching stock and BR rebranding. The latter two items saw the introduction of the ubiquitous BR Mark 1 coaches and the double arrow logo. While dieselisation and electrification were in full flow, the northwest of England remained the last bastion of steam working up until 3rd August 1968 when two trains left Preston on the last standard gauge steam-hauled passenger services in the UK. The occasion is marked with a plaque on the building on platform 4 - see photo opposite.

In 1973 electric traction extended north from Crewe to Preston and a year later the Preston to Glasgow section of the WCML was energised on 25th March 1974 with services starting on 6th May 1974. The very next day the Queen and the Duke of Edinburgh visited Preston station to unveil a plaque marking the electrification of the WCML from London to Glasgow. After the Royal visit that included stopping by at Preston power box, the Queen and Duke travelled on a Preston to Glasgow service as far as Lancaster on the newly electrified line. This occasion is marked by a small plaque bolted on almost as an afterthought it seems to an OLE stanchion again on platform 4 - see below. Services from Preston to Blackpool North and Preston to Bolton and Manchester were not electrified until 2018 and 2019, respectively.

Modernisation of the railways continued and by the 1990s the Preston - Lancaster route saw a mix of Regional Railways and InterCity trains. InterCity in its heyday used class 86, 87 and 90 locomotives hauling Mark 3 coaches on Euston to Glasgow services. Prior to electrification north of Preston in 1974 trains were usually hauled by class 50 diesels, often double-headed. In the late 1960s, BR began experiments with their Advanced Passenger Train (APT) but the scheme was not successful and the APTs were withdrawn but the technology survived. It was sold to Fiat Ferroviaria and used to develop class 390 Pendolinos and class 221 Super Voyagers that are seen on the WCML today.

Inset above: Shot on 5th May 2022, this plaque on platform 4 commemorates the 50th anniversary of the end of steam traction on BR. (Roy Davies)

The next milestone to affect services on the route was privatisation enabled by the Railways Act 1993 that saw franchises awarded to various Train Operating Companies (TOCs), including those seen on the Preston-Lancaster route.

The WCML franchise was operated by Virgin Trains (VT) from 9th March 1997; later replaced by Avanti West Coast from 8th December 2019. Inter-regional express services were launched by BR in the 1990s and operated by various franchisees, including Virgin CrossCountry, culminating with services transferred to First TransPennine Express on 1st February 2004 and to TransPennine Express (TPE) from 1st April 2016 and will run until 31st March 2023, with an option to extend for two years. Prior to privatisation, local services were the domain of North West Regional Railways and from 2nd March 1997 the franchise was awarded to Great Western Holdings trading as North Western Trains. This TOC was rebranded First North Western in November 1998 and services continued until 11th December 2004. On the following day, franchisee, Serco-Abellio, operated services as Northern Rail until 31st March 2016 and from the next day Arriva Trains operated the service under an agreement scheduled to run until March 2025. The franchise experienced a

Inset below: Bolted on to an OLE stanchion this plaque, also on platform 4, commemorates the electrification of the WCML from Preston to Glasgow. (Roy Davies)

This plaque was unveiled by the Queen on the occasion of the visit of Her Majesty and the Duke of Edinburgh on 7th May 1974 to mark the final stage of electrifying the railway from London to Glasgow

number of operational problems from which it could not recover and so Northern was taken over on 1st March 2020 by publicly-owned Northern Trains. Avanti West Coast owned by FirstGroup (70%) and Trenitalia (30%) began operating WCML services replacing VT on 8th December 2019.

From 2023, state-owned Great British Railways (GBR) will oversee rail transport across the UK and under the new arrangement TOCs will become subcontractors to GBR rather than franchisees.

On 1st October 1873, the Caledonian Railway introduced a LNWR sleeping car on mail trains three days per week between Glasgow and London via the WCML and sleeper trains have continued to run on the WCML since then. Responsibility for operation of the Anglo-Scottish services passed within British Rail from InterCity West Coast to ScotRail on 5th March 1995. The overnight service was relaunched as the Caledonian Sleeper from 4th June 1996. On 31st March 1997, it became part of the ScotRail franchise operated initially by National Express. Locomotives were hired from Virgin Trains until March 1998 when English, Welsh and Scottish Railway (EWS) took on the contract. Serco Caledonian Sleepers took over the operation of the train on 31st March 2015 and entered into an agreement with GB Railfreight to hire class 92s for the WCML section.

The WCML is one of the busiest mixed-traffic railway routes in Europe, carrying not only a significant number of passenger services as highlighted above, but, as one of the busiest freight routes in Europe, it carries 40% of all UK rail freight much of which traverses the Preston - Lancaster section. From the start of the railways in the northwest up until the Transport Act 1962, the train companies had to deal with wagonload freight as well as consists of oil, mineral and coal traffic. By then freight was in decline, particularly wagonload traffic, with much transferring to road haulage. The situation continued until 1982 when BR created the Railfreight sector that saw locomotives branded by oil, mineral and coal divisions, which continued until 1994 when freight passed into private ownership. Six freight operating companies were formed during the period 1994-97, although Network Rail infrastructure services remain in Government ownership. Examples of all can be seen on the Preston - Lancaster route.

Between 1955 and 1995 BR branded 'Motorail' services would have been seen on the Preston-Lancaster route.

Another operator of note on the route is state-owned Direct Rail Services (DRS). Created in 1994, its primary role that continues to this day is the haulage of nuclear flask trains between Sellafield and various power stations around the UK. In 2002 DRS diversified to include general freight services and passenger traffic in 2007.

The Preston - Lancaster route is also host to Royal Mail services between Willesden, Warrington and Shieldmuir, near Motherwell, and for many years a variety of mainline charter services that are seen on the route and are frequently steam-hauled.

Under original plans, there was to be a link between HS2 and the WCML south of Wigan known as the Golborne Spur but it was cancelled by the Government in mid-2022 due to strong objections from those living along the proposed route. The spur would have enabled HS2 trains to serve Wigan and Preston, as well as Lancaster, Cumbria and Scotland with an associated reduction in journey times by allowing HS2 trains to bypass Crewe and the double track bottleneck between Winsford and Weaver Junction. Whether a replacement spur north of Crewe ever gets built is a matter for long-term speculation.

Permitted maximum line speeds on the WCML now stand at up to 110mph (177km/h) for standard trains and 125mph (201km/h) for tilting trains, ie Pendolinos and Super Voyagers, which no doubt would have been something that could not have been imagined or even comprehended when the Preston - Lancaster line was opened in 1840.

PASSENGER SERVICES

Today passengers starting their journey or changing trains at Preston can reach Glasgow, Edinburgh, London, Birmingham, Manchester and various parts of Lancashire, Cumbria, Yorkshire and Merseyside from the station; plus, it is host to the Caledonian Sleeper service to Aberdeen, Inverness and Fort William. Similarly Lancaster, as well as host to trains to/from Preston, offers services to Morecambe and Heysham and via Carnforth to towns and cities in North and West Yorkshire. Prior to World War II there would have been a variety of stopping services on the route, typically for example Morecambe to Preston and intermediate stations. Some of the intermediate stations were closed in 1939 with the final closure being Garstang & Catterall in 1969. Passengers at Lancaster could also reach Morecambe and Heysham via Lancaster Green Ayre until closure of the route in 1966. In addition to mainline services using the route both Preston and Lancaster were host to services from intermediate stations and branch lines, with the exception of Knott End where all services terminated at Garstand & Catterall. All three branch lines ceased passenger operations in 1930.

Bradshaw hotel advertisement, August 1931.

MANCHESTER and LIVERPOOL to WIGAN, PRESTON, LANCASTER, KENDAL, CARLISLE, &c.—London and North Western.

Down. — Week Days. — Sundays.

Fares from Manchester	Down.	Week Days / Sundays
1 cl. 2 cl. 3 cl.		

Stations (Down):

- Victoria Sta., Manchester
- Ordsal Lane
- Eccles
- Patricroft
- Barton Moss
- Astley
- Kenyon Junc.
- Newton Bridge arr
- L'pool (Lime St.)
- (Edge Hill)
- Broad Green
- Roby
- Huyton, fr Preset
- Huyton Quarry
- Rainhill
- Lea Green
- St. Helens Junc.
- Collins Green
- Earlestown Junc.
- 110 LONDON (Eus.)
- 111 BIRMINGHAM
- Warrington
- Newton Bridge
- Preston Junction
- Golborne
- M'chester (Vic)
- Ordsal Lane
- Cross Lane
- Weaste
- Eccles
- Wigan 138, 210
- Standish [206]
- Coppull
- Euxton 209
- Leyland
- Farington [214, 222]
- Preston 208, 212
- M'chests (Vic.)
- L'pool (Exchg.)
- Preston dep
- Barton & Broughton
- Brock
- Garstang
- Scorton
- Bay Horse
- Galgate
- LEEDS 174 dep
- BRADFORD 174
- Lancaster 175
- Hest Bank 153
- Bolton-le-Sands
- Carnforth 136, 175
- Burton and Holm
- Milnthorpe [133
- Kendal J. (Oxnhlm)
- KENDAL 133 arr
- WINDRMERE arr
- Grayrigg
- LEEDS 174 dep
- BRADFORD 174
- Ingleton dep
- Kirkby Lonsdle
- Barbon
- Middleton
- Sedbergh
- Low Gill Junc.
- Tebay 183 ar
- Low Gill Junction
- Tebay Junction 183
- Shap
- Clifton 182
- Penrith 137
- Plumpton
- Calthwaite
- Southwte [182, 137
- Wreay [216, 217
- Carlisle 228, 218
- EDINBRO' 228 arr
- GLASGOW 229
- PERTH 229
- 235 INVERNESS
- 232 ABERDEEN

Bradshaw,
June 1869

Bradshaw hotel advertisement, July 1903.

PRESTON

Located almost exactly halfway between Euston and Glasgow Central on the WCML, Preston was always an important interchange station virtually from the outset. By the early 1880s no fewer than nine different lines ran into Preston, although it was not until 1900 that all lines into the town shared a single station and the various companies had been taken over by one or both of the LNWR and L&YR. Today passengers can reach London in the south, Inverness in the north, Blackpool and Merseyside in the west and Yorkshire to the east. Preston is also a staging post for driver changeover particularly on the Anglo-Scottish inter-city and Royal Mail services; additionally TransPennine Express has a drivers' depot at Preston; formerly that used by Virgin CrossCountry.

↑ *Inset: A photo of the former East Lancs (L&Y) entrance taken after closure on 15th February 1975. The building was later demolished as Butler Street was widened westwards. (N.D. Mundy)*

1. An exterior view down the ramp to the former LNWR entrance to Preston station c1974. The building itself is Grade II listed. The canopy along the length of the lower level of the building protected passengers from the elements when alighting from their horse-drawn carriages. This was finally removed in the late 1980s. The ramp continues inside past the booking office down to platforms 3 and 4. Other platforms are reached via footbridges or underpasses. There is also a side entrance to the station on Butler Street that reached the final stages of an architectural competition, the Carbuncle Cup, not for the best but the worst new building. It lost out to an office development in London. The original station was rebuilt in 1880 and extended in 1903 and 1913 to accommodate 15 platforms (see map III overleaf). Significant rationalisation was carried out in the early 1970s; see Map IVb, near picture 4. (Lens of Sutton Association 'LOSA')

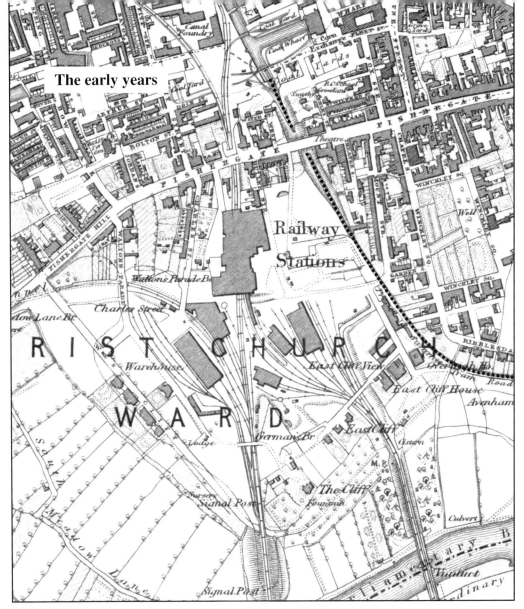

The early years

II. This 1849 6ins map depicts the original NUR station on Butler Street. Note the lines converging to the north of the station towards the short tunnel under Fishergate.

As mentioned earlier, the Bolton & Preston Railway intended to utilise the Lancaster Canal Tram Road - see the dotted line - and have its own station at Preston; accordingly, it reserved a site behind the Victoria Hotel on Fishergate at the southern end of the L&PJR on land occupied by Maxwell House not far from the Dock Street station. 'Maxwell House' station opened on 1st January 1842 and the L&PJR used it from that date. Remnants of the canal tramway remain today: the Old Tram Bridge over the Ribble and the tunnel to the car park under the Fishergate shopping centre. The B&PR was taken over by the NUR in January 1844 and the two agreed to use the Butler Street station.

In 1850 the East Lancashire Railway opened a line from Bamber Bridge to Preston that gave the company a more direct route, which avoided having to use the NUR's line at Farington. The ELR was absorbed by the L&YR on 13th May 1859. On 26th July 1889 the NUR was jointly absorbed by the LNWR and L&YR that both shared the Butler Street station, which underwent major rebuilding in 1880.

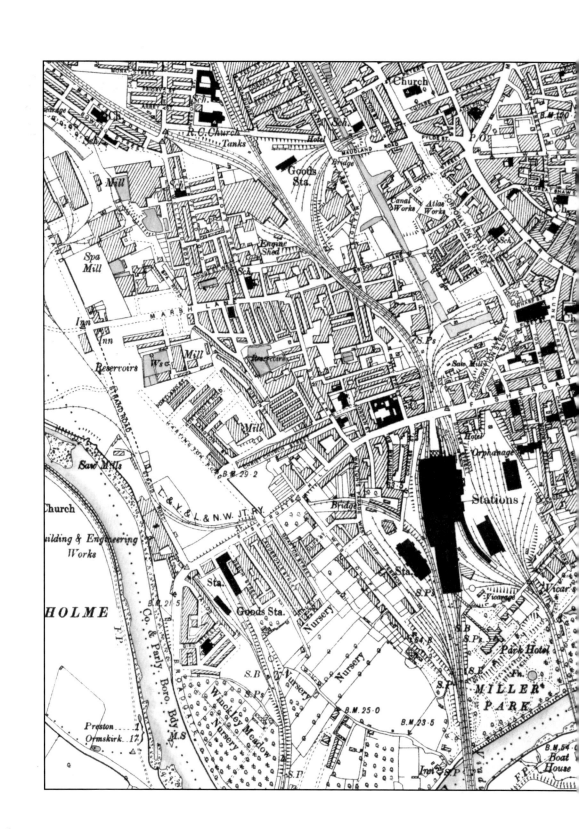

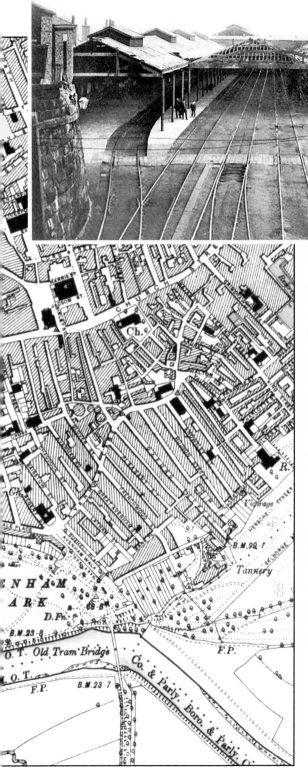

↑   2. A very early shot of the station, which opened in 1838, taken around 1860 from Fishergate looking south before being totally rebuilt in 1880. Note the dilapidated state of the building. With no footbridges, passengers had to cross the lines at track level. The tracks begin to converge at the north end of the station so they could pass under Fishergate by way of a tunnel - the same tunnel that L&PJR passengers had to walk through when avoiding the sixpence surcharge for riding over NUR metals from Dock Street to the Butler Street station. It is reported that over half a million passengers used this decrepit facility during the guild week of 1862. (Harris Library)

The first major rebuild

III. This 1895 6ins map shows the station rebuilt in 1880 with the LNWR and L&YR lines sharing the Butler Street station. To the west is the Fishergate Hill Station that served the West Lancashire Railway (WLR). The tunnel under Fishergate had gone by then being replaced by a viaduct that can be seen today but did require several buildings to be demolished.

3. Fishergate Hill opened on 15th September 1882 as the terminus of the WLR direct link from Southport to Preston. It closed to passengers on 16th July 1900 when the WLR was absorbed by the L&YR. From that date passenger traffic was transferred to the Butler Street station (East Lancs platforms). In this undated photograph empty coaching stock is stabled at the station. It remained open for goods traffic until 25th January 1965 and saw occasional passenger specials. One such excursion was the 13.10 1X23 Fishergate goods station to Grassington on 22nd September 1962; LNWR G2 'Super D' 0-8-0 no. 49451 worked it from Fishergate to Longridge and back to Preston East Lancs. One of the class remains in the National Railway Museum's National Collection. (John Alsop coll.)

→ IVa. This 1912 map shows the extent the station was modified to incorporate the East Lancs lines and the river crossings associated with the station, including the tram bridge. Platform details are given in map IVb, overleaf. By this time Fishergate had closed to passenger traffic.

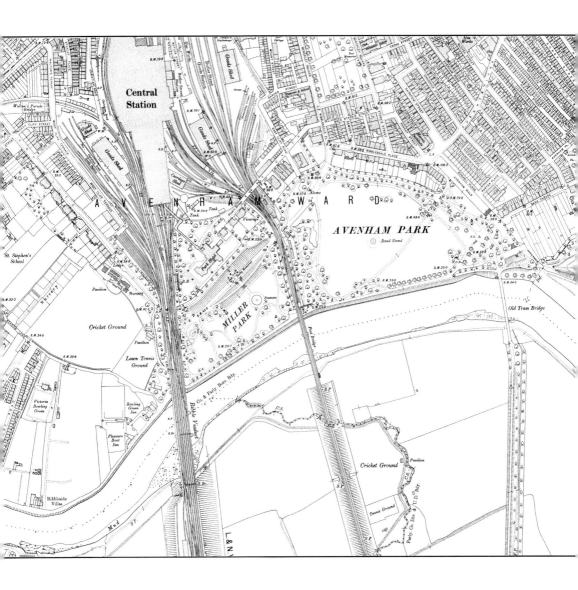

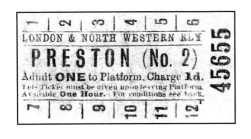

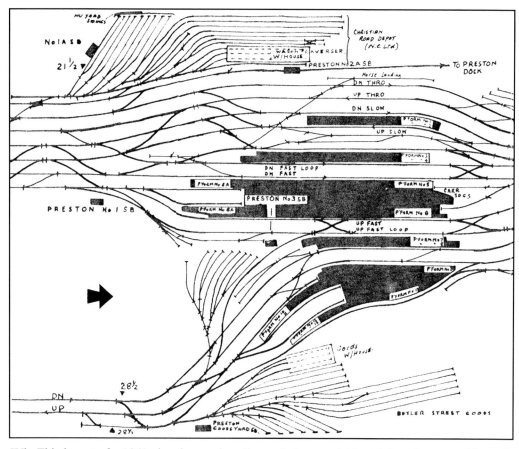

IVb. This is part of a 1969 plan, known in railway circles as a 'side strip', and was used by train planning staff and general use by operating staff. It shows the complexity of the station following the 1880 rebuild and subsequent alterations and modifications. Platforms 1 and 2 forming a large island platform were added in 1903. Platforms 5 and 6 (now 3 and 4 respectively) formed the main wide island platform with a full set of buildings along its centre used mainly for WCML services. At the south end of platforms 5 and 6 are two bay platforms, the Wigan bays, used for both passenger traffic and formerly parcels vans. (Ron Herbert)

Hotel advertisement, *Bradshaw* July 1910.

4.   This aerial shot of Preston station was taken from the south in 1948. Bottom right is the Park Hotel (seen in pictures 7 and 13) and above are the East Lancs platforms and goods sheds (picture 9 and inset). In the centre is the former LNWR station with an overall roof (picture 5). Top left, at Fylde Junction, is St Walburge Church (picture 48) and left centre are the Christian Road goods sidings. (National Collection of Aerial Photography, *ncap.org.uk*)

The southern approaches to the station

5. This c1920 view of the station is in LNWR times. The main canopy is as built in the 1880s and extended over all LNWR platforms, including the two south-facing (Wigan) bays. The canopy was later cut back 150ft and removed completely from the west side of the station. To the right can be seen the glass bridge that allowed passengers access to the Park Hotel from platform 6 - now platform 4. (John Alsop coll.)

6. On 6th April 1964 Riddles WD class 2-8-0 no. 90720 passes Preston EL goods signal box working the Lostock Hall local trip, conveying one container and a brakevan; the local Permanent Way gang can be seen working on the down line. Below the line is Avenham Park, the River Ribble and the former tram road bridge, now a pedestrian crossing is in the background. The line continued to be open until the closure of the East Lancs side of the station and closure of the line toward Todd Lane Junction, Bamber Bridge and Lostock Hall Junction. The WD 2-8-0 was a long-time resident of Lostock Hall MPD up to its withdrawal in July 1965. (Ron Herbert)

7. On 23rd April 1962, with the former Park Hotel in the background, the fireman of Stanier class 4 2-6-4T no. 42436 trims the coal on the bunker; a task which could not be undertaken now because of high voltage OLE. The locomotive, seen working on the former East Lancs line, was allocated to Lostock Hall shed and spent its entire life there until withdrawal in May 1966. Note the former glass bridge over the covered wagons is in the background. (Noel Machell)

8. Stanier Black 5 4-6-0 no. 45236 on one of the through lines on 8th January 1967. Note the train is approaching the remains of the glass bridge referred to earlier. (*ColourRail.com*)

9. On 21st August 1964 BR 2-6-0 no. 78041 is seen departing Preston working the 13.25 Preston to Southport from bay platform 12 with a Stanier 2-6-4T stood in platform 10, also a bay. Platform 13 can be seen on the right, which was a through platform. The connecting line from platform 7 can also be seen on the left. This was used on Sundays, when Midge Hall Junction was closed. The L&Y goods warehouse is seen on the right and two larger L&Y warehouses were further to the right and out of sight. In the background, over the station roof, the top of the former East Lancs station building at street level can just be seen - see inset to picture no. 1. (Ron Herbert)

10. While on holiday in Cumbria, the photographer bought a day return ticket to Preston on 19th April 1968. He took this shot of BR 'Britannia' 4-6-2 no. 70013 *Oliver Cromwell*, which travelled from the north light engine and ran into the East Lancs side of the station. The Butler Street Goods depot is in the background. It is assumed the engine was on its way from Carnforth to Lostock Hall MPD. (Gordon Edgar)

Inset: One of the two larger warehouses referred to in the previous caption was recorded on 15th June 1983. The writing on the roof reads: 'Lancashire and Yorkshire Railway Goods Warehouse'. The two large warehouses were demolished sometime after the photograph was taken to make way for the Fishergate shopping centre opened in the 1980s together with its car park and the current station car park. (Ron Herbert)

↓   11. An unexpected bonus for the enthusiasts waiting to travel on the RCTS 'Duchess Commemorative Rail Tour' on 5th October 1963 was the sight of another member of the class, no. 46241 *City of Edinburgh*, heading south out of Preston station with 2K82, the 06.15 Carlisle to Crewe stopping train. The photograph was taken from the partially demolished glass bridge. The modern block behind the Wigan Bays was built in the mid-1960s to connect the GPO sorting office in Christian Road with the station via a continuous overhead track which the mail bags were hooked on to. (Noel Machell)

12.   Fowler Class 4F 0-6-0 No. 44060 of 12A Kingmoor MPD passes through Preston hauling three Stanier Class 5s Nos.45012 of 12B Carlisle Upperby, 45112 and 45481 also of 12A MPD enroute from Carlisle to Crewe Works on 19th March 1963. The former GPO mechanised bridge that housed the continuous overhead track as mentioned in the previous caption can be clearly seen; it has since been removed. (Ron Herbert)

13. Formed of BR Mark II coaching stock, a Manchester to Glasgow train heads towards platform 6 at Preston station on a Saturday afternoon in April 1983. The locomotive in charge of the train, a class 47/4 no. 47518, will be detached and replaced by a 25KV Electric locomotive for the remainder of the journey to Glasgow. The former railway-owned Park Hotel above the locomotive was a prominent landmark at the southern end of the station. (Noel Machell)

14. On 14th April 1991 a batch of class 87s stand in the North Union electric holding sidings awaiting their next tour of duty, which was usually heading south on both freight and passenger services. The North Union electric holding sidings were originally a marshalling yard and only became the holding sidings following the electrification of the WCML. (Ron Herbert)

15. During a day of what proved to be incessant rainfall, Northern Rail class 153 Super Sprinter no. 153378 heads away from the Wigan bays forming the 12.35 service to Ormskirk on 17th June 2015. (Gordon Edgar)

16. An undated early photograph of platform 3 (originally no. 5), left, and platform 2 (originally no. 4). (John Alsop coll.)

17. In this undated photograph LNWR Claughton class 4-6-0 no. 695 *Sir Arthur Lawley* stands in platform 4 (originally no. 6) with a southbound express. (London North Western Railway Society)

18. On 25th April 1951, station pilot ex-Wirral, ex-LMS Aspinall 2-4-2T no. 46762 is propelling its train north out of platform 1, the correct direction of travel. It is displaying Station Pilot head lamps which explains why it is travelling in reverse. (H.C.Casserley)

19. Stanier Coronation class 8P 4-6-2 no. 46240 *City of Coventry* arrives at the former platform 2 working 3K16 8.15am Carlisle to Crewe parcels on 8th June 1964 a few months before its withdrawal. Bridge 129 (Fishergate Bridge) can be seen along with Preston No 4 signal box in the background. Built in 1940 as a streamlined loco based at Camden (1B), the casing was removed after the end of WWII. (Ron Herbert)

↑ 20. Magnificently lit by the station illumination every detail of the overall roof and the loco-motive and its train standing at platform 4 is revealed. This scene was photographed at 7.40pm on a clear November evening in 2001. The train is a Glasgow - Euston working propelled by BR class 87 no. 87008 *City of Liverpool*; the DVT at the head of the train was not identified. The locomotive was one of the batch exported to Bulgaria after displacement by BR class 390 Pendolinos on Virgin WCML duties (Noel Machell)

21. A class 108 DMU stands at platform 2 one evening in November 1981 awaiting to depart to Colne. The foreground railings protect the stairwell serving the subway giving access to all platforms; additionally there is a second subway accessed only by lifts where original parts of the station masonry and brickwork can be observed. (Noel Machell)

22. Resplendent in Virgin CrossCountry livery BR Diesel class 43 power car no. 43068 pauses in platform 4 at the head of an Edinburgh to Birmingham train in August 1997. (Noel Machell)

23. A view across platform 4 looking towards platform 5 on the 17th October 2007 finds BR class 185 diesel-hydraulic Desiro unit no. 185109 forming a Trans PennineExpress service from Blackpool North to Manchester Airport. Adjacent is a class 221 Super Voyager no. 221128 with the Virgin CrossCountry Bournemouth to Edinburgh train. (Noel Machell)

24. Finished in the original 'Merseyrail' yellow and white livery with a black waistband, class 142 'Pacer' unit no. 142054 stands in platform 5 awaiting its next turn of duty on the evening of 26th January 1998. The night-time station lighting illuminates the structure of the high overall roof to very good effect. Despite being truly disliked by many passengers, thirty of the class 142 units have been preserved with a further seven retained in industrial use; the unit in this photograph not having been so favoured. (Noel Machell)

25. BR class 92 GB Railfreight Co-Co dual-voltage electric locomotive no. 92033 stands at Preston (northbound - pick up and southbound - set down only) around 04.30 on 30th May 2015 and is about to set off for Euston with 1M16 Highland sleeper service from Inverness, Aberdeen and Fort William. (Andrewstransport)

← *Inset: The latest Caledonian Sleeper livery was applied to a few Mark 3 coaches before they were replaced by the Mark 5s built by CAF. Here is Mark 2 no. 9802 (seating) seen on the same day. (Andrewstransport)*

26. BR diesel-electric Co-Co class 60 no. 60021 *Pen-y-Ghent* and BR class 92 no. 92033 *Railway Heritage Trust* on 1S25 at Preston on 17th June 2022 at 01.32. This extraordinary sight of the Caledonian Sleeper being hauled by the class 60 from Warrington Bank Quay was because of OLE damage on the down WCML at Coppull, caused by BR electro-diesel class 88 no. 88010 on the 4S44 service the previous day. (Andrewstransport)

27. After a night of heavy rainfall, the low winter morning sunlight bathes platform 4 south end as Freightliner BR class 70 Co-Co no. 70015 powers through in charge of the 04.28 Coatbridge to Daventry intermodal on 7th February 2017. (Gordon Edgar)

28. Northern Trains 'Civity' class 195/1 DMU no. 195125 pauses in platform 5, while working from Manchester Airport to Barrow-in-Furness, on 23rd October 2019 only a few months after introduction of the fleet in July. The Spanish manufacturer, CAF, produces a variety of commuter and regional trains for the global market based on its modular 'Civity' platform including classes 195 DMUs and 331 EMUs for Northern Trains. Given the number of passengers on platform 4, it looks like a London-bound inter-city service is imminent. (Mark Bartlett)

Going north

29. LNWR Improved Precedent class 2-4-0 no. 265 *Thomas Carlyle* seen departing platform 3 with an unidentified train for the North in 1914. The overall roof canopy extended northwards as part of the 1903 station improvements but was removed in the early 1950s. (LNWR Society)

30. LMS Stanier Coronation class 4-6-2 no. 6222 *Queen Mary* departs for the north in April 1939. This locomotive had the distinction of being modelled by Hornby in 1986. (PDA/Roger Davis)

← 31. Ex-LMS Stanier Black 5s nos 45033 and 44761 double head the down 'Mid-Day Scot' as it arrives in platform 5 (now platform 3) on 5th June 1959. Note the station pilot beneath the signal gantry and vans in the Wigan Bays. (*ColourRail.com*/W. Ashcroft)

← 32. Right on the strike of 10.00am on Saturday 5th October 1963, ex-LMS 'Princess Coronation' pacific no. 46251 *City of Nottingham* coasts to a stop to pick up passengers for the 'Duchess Commemorative' rail tour organised by the Lancashire and North West Branch of the RCTS. The tour gave enthusiasts the chance of travelling behind one of these powerful locomotives on a return trip from Crewe to Edinburgh (Princes St.), the *City of Nottingham* was acting as a substitute for the planned use of 46256 *Sir William A Stanier* which had developed a bogie defect shortly before the tour. (Noel Machell)

↑ 33. Gresley A4 4-6-2 no. 60019 *Bittern* working the 05.00 light engine Stockport to Aberdeen Ferryhill MPD on 9th March 1966 is seen standing in platform 1. She had been sent south to work 1T70 Special on 6th March 1966 from Manchester Piccadilly to Crewe and Derby works and returned to Manchester the same day. With the introduction of the A4s by the LNER from 1935, the LMS was persuaded to streamline its newly designed Coronation class. The first 10 were streamlined but due to operational and maintenance issues the streamlining was removed after WWII. De-streamlining began in 1946 with the last, *City of Lancaster*, in May 1949. Preston No. 4 signal box can be seen under the Fishergate bridge No 129. (Ron Herbert)

34. In this undated photo in the 1960s Black 5 no. 45287 heads a relief train to Blackpool out of platform 1 seen passing an ex-LNWR wooden signal post that was clearly built to last. (Michael Ellis)

35. On 2nd August 1981 class 86 no. 86321 is passing through platform 3 on 1S55 the 12.10 Kensington Olympia - Perth Motorail service; sister locomotive no. 86212 is stood in the Derby siding and an unidentified class 47 is in the Bakehouse siding. The OLE stops short of the two sidings. (Ron Herbert)

36.   On 15th May 2018 English Electric Type 3 BR class 37/4 Co-Co no. 37402 is about to depart from platform 4 on a Cumbrian coast service in its last week. This locomotive has a history of name changes: 1985 *Oor Wullie*; 1993 unnamed; 1994 *Bont Y Bermo* and 2013 *Stephen Middlemore 23.12.1954 - 8.6.2013* in memory of a DRS Railways Safety and Train Officer, who was tragically killed in 2013. (Jonathan Dixon)

Off-Peak Day Return   D   Return

Valid for one journey   Date of travel
from Preston (Lancs)   05-MAY-22
to   Lancaster

See restrictions nre.co.uk/B3
Adult Standard Class
with Senior Railcard
Refundable and exchangeable for a fee

£5.60X   23901-3090-8947-10-05-00

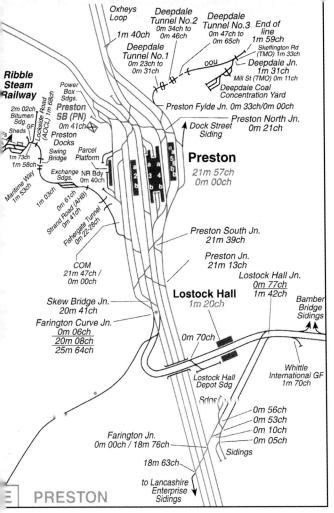

Ribble Steam Railway

Oxheys Loop

Deepdale Tunnel No.2
0m 34ch to
0m 46ch
1m 40ch

Deepdale Tunnel No.3
0m 47ch to
0m 65ch

End of line
1m 59ch

Skeffington Rd (TMO) 1m 33ch

Deepdale Tunnel No.1
0m 23ch to
0m 31ch

oou

Deepdale Jn.
1m 31ch

Mill St (TMO) 0m 11ch

Deepdale Coal Concentration Yard

Preston Fylde Jn. 0m 33ch/0m 00ch

Preston North Jn.
0m 21ch

Power Box Sdgs.

Preston SB (PN)
0m 41ch

2m 02ch
Bitumen Sdg.
GF

Lockside Road (AOCL) 1m 68ch

Sheds

Preston Docks

Swing Bridge

Dock Street Siding

Parcel Platform

NR Bdy
0m 40ch

Preston
21m 57ch
0m 00ch

1m 73ch
1m 58ch

Maritime Way
1m 53ch

Exchange Sdgs.

1m 03ch

0m 61ch

Strand Road (AHB)
0m 41ch

Fishergate Tunnel
0m 22-28ch

COM
21m 47ch /
0m 00ch

Preston South Jn.
21m 39ch

Preston Jn.
21m 13ch

Lostock Hall Jn.
0m 77ch
1m 42ch

Skew Bridge Jn.
20m 41ch

Lostock Hall
1m 20ch

Bamber Bridge Sidings

Faringale Curve Jn.
0m 06ch
20m 08ch
25m 64ch

0m 70ch

Whittle International GF
1m 70ch

Lostock Hall Depot Sdg

Sdgs

Faringale Jn.
0m 00ch / 18m 76ch

0m 56ch
0m 53ch
0m 10ch
0m 05ch

Sidings

18m 63ch

to Lancashire Enterprise Sidings

E **PRESTON**

1970s rationalisation

V. The 1970s rationalisation saw a reduction from 13 to six bi-directional platforms with the East Lancs platforms being removed completely. The former platform 1 was lengthened for parcels use. In the eastern side of the station, the up and down goods loop passes the disused platform sometimes referred to by railway staff as platform 9 - its former number. It contains bicycle racks, luggage lockers and provides access to the station car park. The coal depot in Deepdale Street, served by the railway, did not close until the 1990s. (©TRACKmaps)

37. This view of the west side of the station, taken on 15th March 1971, shows the removal of the up and down through lines used by both passenger and freight traffic. The line on the right through former platform 1 was severed to make north and south bays. The centre section was removed to allow road vehicles to access the parcel concentration depot from Christian Road, although no longer used by parcels vehicles. The long through parcel line to the far right of the former platform 2 is still there today but not used by passenger trains. (Ron Herbert)

↑ 38. Deserted East Lancs platforms on 4th July 1972 shortly before demolition. (H.C.Casserley)

➜ 39. Taken on 5th May 2022 above platform 6 is a view of what was formerly platform 9, which retains its curved end revealing its past as one of the East Lancs through platforms. (Roy Davies)

Photographs and memories

The WCML was a major north - south route for troops during both World Wars. The station buffet served free drinks and snacks at cost price to anyone in uniform throughout WWI. Working 24 hours a day some three million service men and women were served between 1915 and 1918 and an estimated 35 million cups of tea were served between 1939 and 1945.

PRESTON STATION FREE BUFFET 1915 to 1919

"You all dwell in the minds of the forces who have had the pleasure of your most comfortable Buffet in Preston."

THE WEEK BEFORE CHRISTMAS 1916 NEARLY 12,500 MEN WERE SERVED IN 36 HOURS

THE PRESTON PALS
TO COMMEMORATE THE MEN OF 'D' COMPANY THE 7TH (SERVICE) BATTALION OF THE LOYAL NORTH LANCASHIRE REGIMENT
19TH WESTERN DIVISION WHO SERVED THEIR COUNTRY WITH HONOUR AND SACRIFICE IN THE GREAT WAR 1914-1918

40a. The walls in the waiting room between platforms 3 and 4, formerly the WWI buffet, are adorned with murals commemorating its illustrious past. (Roy Davies)

↗ 40b. Prominent on the wall between platforms 3 and 4 is the memorial to the volunteers known as the 'Preston Pals' who gave their lives in WWI. (Roy Davies)

DURING THE GREAT WAR OF 1914-1919 THIS ROOM WAS, BY THE PERMISSION OF THE L.&N.W. AND L.&Y. RAILWAY COMPANIES, OCCUPIED FROM AUG.19.1915 TO NOV.11.1919, BY THE PRESTON STATION SAILORS AND SOLDIERS FREE BUFFET ASSOCIATION OF VOLUNTARY WORKERS, WHO SUPPLIED THREE AND A QUARTER MILLIONS OF THE SAILORS AND SOLDIERS WHO PASSED THROUGH THIS STATION, WITH REFRESHMENTS AND COMFORTS. THE ROOM FROM AUG.19.1915 TO MAY 31.1919 WAS OPEN CONTINUOUSLY DAY AND NIGHT AND FROM JUNE 1.1919 TO NOV.11.1919 FOR FOURTEEN HOURS EACH DAY

"Eh, Lads, have any of you been to Preston Station? That's the place where they look after you. "

"Will you please convey our thanks to the ladies of Preston Station who gave up their time to supply us with refreshments which was much appreciated by all."

41. Black Five no. 45025 is at the head of the final steam-hauled Heysham - Manchester Victoria Belfast Boat Express on 5th May 1968. The locomotive has been preserved and runs as 5025 in LMS black lined livery on the Strathspey Railway at Aviemore. (Michael Ellis)

42. The 'Royal Scot Golden Jubilee 1927-1977' special charter train on 2nd May 1977 pauses at Preston headed by an immaculately turned out class 87 no. 87003. The traction inspector, the late Doug Cullen, wearing the traditional bowler hat receives quick instruction on how to use a dignitary's camera. The locomotive was named *Patriot* in 1978 and exported to Bulgaria in 2009. (Gordon Edgar)

A diversity of views past and present

43. Activity on the horse siding c1914. The horse loading dock can be seen between the through lines and the Preston Dock branch on the extreme west side of the station - see map IVb. The houses to the left are on Christian Road that would have allowed vehicular and, in this case, hoof access to the platform. (PDA)

44. BR class 47 no. 47598 stands at the north end of the up and down goods loop on 5th May 1984 waiting to replace class 86 no. 86215 on a Crewe to Barrow-in-Furness train for the onward part of the journey as the Cumbrian coast line was not and is not electrified. To the left of the locomotive is the former through line to the erstwhile platform 13 on the East Lancs side; it was blocked off and the line lifted as Butler Street was extended westwards in the 1970s. It is interesting to note the legend, LMS Preston Station, in the brickwork of the main East Lancs entrance 36 years since it ceased to exist - see the inset alongside picture no. 1. The building was demolished when Butler Street was extended westwards. (Noel Machell)

45. A hybrid 3 car DMU led by a class 108 driving unit enters platform 2 on a Saturday afternoon in April 1983 with a train from Blackpool North bound for Manchester Victoria. Note the sleeping car berthed in the Derby siding at the north end of platform 3; some sleeping cars were dropped at Preston where passengers could sleep in until 07.30. It is rumoured that Lord Derby stabled his saloon at that location but there is no evidence to suggest this was the case. Note the diesel shunter beyond the sleeping car and the electric locomotive beyond in the Bakehouse siding. The photographer was keen to point out the young child playing on a luggage trolley in the vicinity of moving trains. (Noel Machell)

Inset: To the left of the sleeping car in the previous photo, the broad slope down to the main station entrance is clearly visible as are the arches and doors in the brickwork, as seen on 5th May 2022. Those doors lead to a short tunnel housing the end of the Bakehouse siding where locomotives are stored occasionally. (Roy Davies)

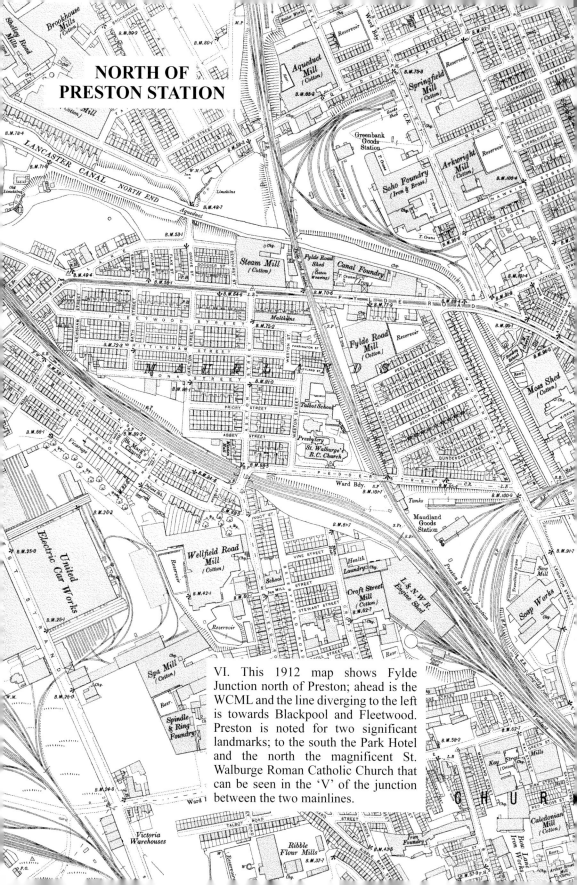

VI. This 1912 map shows Fylde Junction north of Preston; ahead is the WCML and the line diverging to the left is towards Blackpool and Fleetwood. Preston is noted for two significant landmarks; to the south the Park Hotel and the north the magnificent St. Walburge Roman Catholic Church that can be seen in the 'V' of the junction between the two mainlines.

46. On 16th August 1981 a group of BR class 86 25kV electric locomotives are stabled in the Pitt Street sidings immediately to the north of Fishergate with Lancashire County Hall in the background. Normally locomotives working north of Preston were stabled in the Bakehouse or the Derby sidings but in busy times electric locomotives were stabled also in Pitt Street, two sidings just north of the then parcels concentration depot. (Ron Herbert).

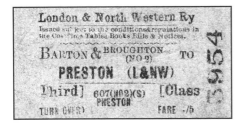

47. Prior to colour-light signalling, another landmark north of the station was the impressive signal gantry located about 100m north of Preston No. 4 signal box. English Electric BR class 50 Co-Co locomotives were the mainstay of express passenger trains on the then non-electrified section of the WCML between Crewe and Scotland. On 21st December 1970 class 50s D401 and D443 are seen heading 1S57 10.05 from Euston to Glasgow Central. In 1978 the locomotives were named *Dreadnought* and *Eagle* respectively and by then had already received their TOPS numbers 50001 and 50043. (Ron Herbert)

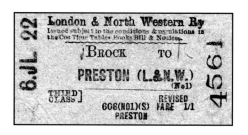

48. St. Walburge is famous as having the tallest spire of any parish church in England. This Ron Herbert shot is taken from the footplate of BR Standard 'Britannia' class 7 No. 70013 *Oliver Cromwell* departing Preston on 1L25 10.40 Euston to Carlisle on 3rd March 1966. The former Motive Power Depot can be see beyond the signal gantry and is now the location of the Preston Power Box. *Oliver Cromwell* became a preservation star after withdrawal in 1968 and in 2018 it was moved to the Great Central Railway; in 2019 it began a major overhaul on the heritage railway. (Ron Herbert)

49. Preston motive power depot (10B) seen here in 1948 was located to the west of the main lines and sidings between the station on the approach to Fylde junction. On shed are ex-LMS Patriot 4-6-0 no. 45516 *The Bedfordshire and Hertfordshire Regiment* and Black Five no. 45020, which was the first of the class to be built at Vulcan Foundry in 1934. The third locomotive cannot be identified but it could be an ex-LMS 2-4-2T; the type used on station pilot duties. (PDA)

50. On 28th June 1960 the roof of Preston shed was destroyed by fire, but the walls and roof beams remained intact. In this shot of 22nd May 1961 the newly exposed shed meant locos found little shelter from the elements such as 'Super D' 7F 0-8-0 no. 49104 whose tender is visible on the left and Thompson B1 4-6-0 no. 61201, which appears to have come in on a special working - probably a Blackpool turn. Preston shed closed in September 1961 its duties then being taken over by Lostock Hall. Preston MPD continued to store withdrawn locos until the remaining buildings were demolished in 1966. (Keith Lewcock)

VII. This map of 1893 shows the Lancashire Canal basin and the Marsh Lane Bridge as illustrated in the following pictures; by then the original tram road - see Map II - had been taken up. Ladywell House was built on the site of the canal basin. The canal now terminates at Shelley Road near Fylde Road less than a mile from the former terminus at Dock Street.

51. The horse boat *Express* is taking on coal at the tipper in the canal basin c1922. Note the pronounced dip in the railway line looking north as it drops below Marsh Lane bridge in the distance. (PDA/Janet Rigby)

Inset: An undated shot of the canal basin now derelict taken from the Marsh Lane Bridge looking south. (PDA)

52. This view looking south on 2nd August 1981 shows Ladywell House and the former Dock Street diesel sidings. Ladywell House was the Divisional HQ for the Preston division that ran from Euxton Junction (Leyland) to Gretna Junction, Carnforth to Carlisle via Barrow and Workington, former L&Y main line from Rochdale up to Hebden Bridge, Carnforth to Settle Junction, plus Skipton to Carlisle via the Settle and Carlisle line and branches to Blackpool, Morecambe and Windermere. It also housed various operating sections for both freight and passenger services, accounts, estate management, control office, telegraph office and the divisional civil engineers. Typically the diesel locomotives would replace electric traction on Anglo Scottish services to/ from Manchester and Liverpool, taking over the last leg to Blackpool on services from Euston

and hauling freight trains from Lostock Hall to Carlisle via Blackburn and Hellifield along with local engineers trips etc. Ladywell House was built on the filled in section of the Lancaster Canal and is now student accommodation for the University of Central Lancashire. The Dock Street sidings were severed by the extension of the Preston ring road and a hotel now occupies the site. (Ron Herbert)

Inset: A busy day in the Preston Control Office, Ladywell House 1967. (Ron Herbert)

← 53. All signal boxes in and around Preston were replaced by the Power Box as seen in this shot on 5th May 2022; it stands on the site of the former Motive Power Depot behind sidings north of the station used by TransPennine Express stock if and when its services are cancelled. The box opened on 21st October 1972 in preparation for the introduction of electrification of the WCML etc through to Scotland in 1974. The power box covered an area from Blainscough Sidings between Wigan and Euxton Junction through to Carnforth (WCML), to Salwick on the Blackpool line, Euxton Junction to Blackrod on the Manchester line, Preston to Hebden Bridge, via Blackburn, Rose Grove and Copy Pit and Preston to Midge Hall on the Ormskirk branch, Todmorden to Smithy Bridge and former L&YR main line to Manchester Victoria. The lines to Morecambe and Heysham and from Salwick to Blackpool were controlled by manual boxes until 2012 and 2018, respectively. When the box was first commissioned it had a flat roof that leaked, as seen in the following picture, and was later replaced by the current double hip-ended structure. After its opening in October 1972, the power signal box took control of all operations between Preston and Lancaster in stages between November 1972 and February 1973. (Roy Davies)

↓ 54. A view of Fylde Junction on 31st July 1971 looking back towards Preston Station taken from more or less in front of St. Walburge Church. The Power Box (indicated by an arrow) can be seen behind the cable wagons still with its original flat roof at the time on the site of the former motive power depot. A BR class 47 heads 1S91 for Carlisle and on the right a DMU approaches Preston from Blackpool. On the left above the class 47 is the former Maudland Goods Yard. (Tom Heavyside)

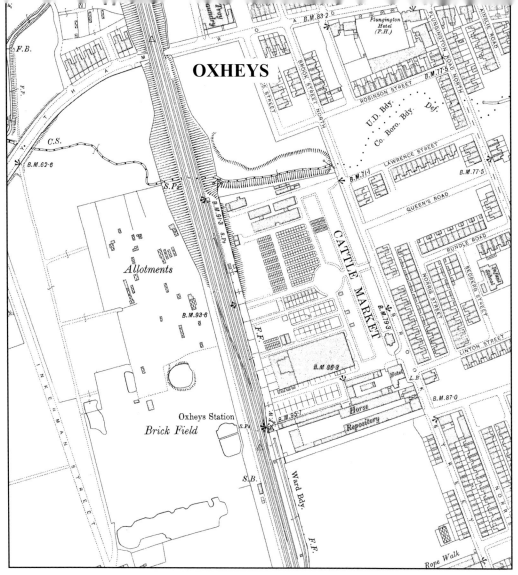

OXHEYS

VIII. Oxheys station was less than half a mile north of Preston station and was opened by the L&PJR in 1869 as a single platform serving Preston Cattle Market on Brook Street. It remained a single platform until closure in 1925. The livestock sidings closed on 9th September 1968 and all that remains today at that location is a passing loop on the up side. This map is dated 1912.

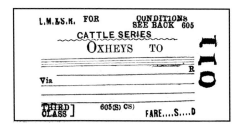

55. Construction of the new arterial road in 1923 required a new bridge over the WCML and here a large section is being lowered into position. The new road was built to give traffic better access to the western suburb of Ashton and onwards to Lytham and Blackpool. It is now known as Blackpool Road and formerly Adison Road. Oxheys signal box can be seen the other side of the bridge to the left; it was built in 1923 to replace the old box dating back to 1902 that had to be demolished to make way for the new bridge. This signal box controlled access to and from the cattle market railway sidings. (London North Western Railway Association 'LNWRA')

56. This view shows the completed bridge and the single platform to the right and the new signal box under the bridge to the left. (LNWRA)

57. The new signal box to the north of the new road controlled access to and from the cattle market sidings. The box closed on 3rd February 1973. (LNWRA)

58. 'Operation Oxheys' was a mock practice exercise performed at the Cattle Market railway sidings. It was a combined operation involving Preston Ambulance, St. John Ambulance, the Fire Service and Civil Defence teams. (St. John Ambulance)

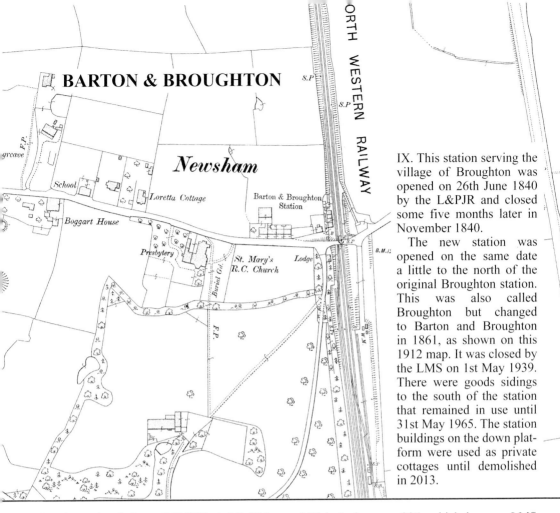

BARTON & BROUGHTON

Newsham

IX. This station serving the village of Broughton was opened on 26th June 1840 by the L&PJR and closed some five months later in November 1840.

The new station was opened on the same date a little to the north of the original Broughton station. This was also called Broughton but changed to Barton and Broughton in 1861, as shown on this 1912 map. It was closed by the LMS on 1st May 1939. There were goods sidings to the south of the station that remained in use until 31st May 1965. The station buildings on the down platform were used as private cottages until demolished in 2013.

59. An undated shot of LNWR 4-6-0 'Prince of Wales' class no. 296, which became LMS no. 5798, hauling an interesting selection of stock. The train is just south of Barton & Broughton where the four track section started. (Edwin Ashworth/Ron Herbert coll.)

60. An undated shot looking south with the entrance to the goods yard on the right past the over bridge (Robert Humm coll.)

61. The main station building has been photographed from the up side c1905. (LOSA)

62. An undated shot after grouping of LNWR 7F 0-8-0 Bowen-Cooke freight locomotive at Barton & Broughton on the up main about to take the up slow line as indicated by the signals in the background. It became 9407 in the new LMS numbering system, although it was still carrying its LNWR number 373 when the photograph was taken shortly after Grouping.
(Edwin Ashworth/Ron Herbert coll.)

63. A Virgin Voyager speeds south past Barton and Broughton Station on 1st May 2009, the 70th Anniversary of the station closing. The building was eventually demolished in 2013. (Mark Bartlett)

ROEBUCK

BROCK

X. Opened by the L&PJR on 26th June 1840, the station (location circled) served the then small village of Bilsborrow but was named after the Roebuck Inn rather than the hamlet itself. The station was replaced by Brock less than a mile further north and was closed in August 1849 but the pub survives to this day. Both this map and the one adjacent are dated 1912.

Ballet Hill

M.P

B.M.109·9

S.P

4 ft. R.H.

Brock Cottage

W.M.

S.P

S.P
Def.
L.B

Brock Statio

S.B.

Parlick Terrace

4 ft. R.H.
C.C.S.

4 ft. R.H.

S.P

4 ft. R.H.

C.C.S.

Tk.B.

Weir

Lashers
F.B.

Lower Bridge
B.M.81·4

Sluice

ospect Villa

Def.

F.P.

S.Ps

LONDON &

← XI. North of Roebuck, the L&PJR opened Brock in August 1849 following closure of the aforementioned station. There was a siding to the west of the line. The River Brock ran under the platforms and the Lancaster Canal to the east. The station was closed by the LMS on 1st May 1939. To the north of the station towards Garstang were water troughs measuring 561yds part of the overall LNWR 300 mile trough network. At this point the WCML is very close to the M6 a little to the east of the former station.

64. A view of the station looking south in around 1912. (LOSA)

65. A view looking north taken in August 1920. (John Alsop coll.)

66. Jubilee 4-6-0 no. 45645 *Collingwood* passes over the Brock water troughs hauling a mixed freight on 9th October 1959. Behind the trees to the right in the picture lies the M6 motorway completed and opened in 1958 part of which was the UK's first motorway otherwise known as the Preston Bypass. (*ColourRail.com*/W. Ashcroft)

→ XII. This station was opened by the L&PJR on 25th June 1840 as Garstang, although it was some 1.5 miles (2.4km) south of the town and closer to the village of Catterall. In 1881 the station was renamed as Garstang and Catterall by the LNWR. On 5th December 1870 it became a junction station when the Garstang & Knott End Railway (GKER) opened a line, although initially only to Pilling. The Knott-End (more common spelling) branch only connected to the main line by way of the goods yard reached via the western side of the down island platform.

Garstang & Catterall station was built on the north side of Ray Lane that passed under the line; the station house was erected on the downside with the Lancaster Canal to the west of the line. The station was also adjacent to the Kenlis Arms Hotel; the building seen on the right of picture no. 67. In 1873 the LNWR gave the station a face lift; in addition to the station house, a large single-storey brick building was erected on the up platform together with a shelter on the down side and a footbridge at its southern end.

On 31st March 1930 passenger services were withdrawn by the LMS between Garstang & Catterall and Knott End but goods services continued. On 13th November 1950 goods services to Knott End were withdrawn but continued as far as Pilling until 1st August 1963, when services were further cut back to Garstang Town. Several years after Garstang & Catterall was listed for closure, goods services ended on 30th December 1968 with complete closure of the station on 3rd February 1969. Today, all is gone apart from the station house, which remains as a private dwelling as does the Kenlis Arms in the foreground. There is an emergency rail crossover at the site of the former station.

GARSTANG & CATTERALL

& NORTH WESTERN RAILWAY

F.P.

F.P.

Lees Farm

Dobson's Bridge

F.P.

Chy.

Tokio Creamery

S.P.

S.P.

Cattle Sale Yd.

KENLIS ROAD

Woodlands

Garstang & Catterall Station

L   a   n   e B.M.67·1

Spring Cottages

B.M.75·8

Kenlis Arms Hotel (P.H.)

Little Calder River

Ray Lane Bridge

W.M.

L.B

S.P.

Bag Factory

Chy.

S.B.

F.P.

F.P.

W.M.

67. A view of the Kenlis Arms hotel and station forecourt c1905 on the up side of the station. The main station building is hidden behind the hotel. The footbridge connects the down island platform that hosted the GKER trains until 1930. (LOSA)

68 A view from the footbridge possibly in 1910 looks north; note the GKER carriages in the bay platform on the extreme left. (Robert Humm coll.)

69. An undated shot of Ivatt 2MT 2-6-0 no. 46421 heading south hauling an elderly arc-roof van. The signal box is an LNWR type C that was opened in the early 1870s coinciding with the commissioning of the Knott End railway as far as Pilling. It closed in November 1972 when the route came under the control of Preston power box. (Robert Humm coll.)

70. Stanier 4-6-0 Black Five no. 45343 (LMS 5343) hauls a van train heading south on 6th April 1957. Note the platform to the left used by trains off the GKER branch; there was no direct access to the mainline other than via the goods yard - see picture no. 72. (Robert Humm coll.)

71. Stanier Black Five no. 45135 is shunting wagons in the goods yard on 25th July 1963. (*ColourRail.com*/W. Ashcroft)

72. A view of the goods yard taken from the footbridge at the south end of the station in around 1952. Access to the mainline from the Knott End branch was via the goods yard only. The double slip indicates the challenge the yard presented to the working of goods traffic. (Cumbrian Railways Association Jackson collection ref JA1016)

73. An undated shot of class 40 no. D334 (TOPS no. 40134 from May 1974) passes the station hauling the up 'Caledonian'. Note the Kenlis Arms in the background that closed on 30th April 2022; a search is on for new owners.
(Cumbrian Railways Association Connop-Price collection ref MCP030)

74. An unidentified class 47 passes the station in August 1967 with the 14.25 Carlisle - Willesden freight service that includes a number of cattle wagons. The white building in the background is Garstang Creamery, which had access to the up siding at one time. It has since been demolished and the land occupied by the Creamery Industrial Estate. (*ColourRail.com*)

75. A Cravens DMU is departing for Lancaster as passengers having alighted head for the foot-bridge. The photo was probably taken in the mid-1960s, so Lancaster would have been the next stop. (Knott End Railway Society)

76. TransPennine Express 5-car (bi-modal) BMU class 802s took over some Edinburgh to Manchester Airport services from May 2022. These were designated Nova 1 trainsets by TPE. Here we see no. 802216 crossing the Grizedale Beck, just to the north of Garstang & Catterall station, at the site of the former Woodacre crossing heading south on 27th June 2022. The M6 motorway is behind the trees seen on the right. (Mark Bartlett)

Inset: Taken from more or less the same spot nearly 60 years earlier with the Woodacre crossing and gatekeepers cottages still in place. Black 5 4-6-0 no. 45013 is on a south-bound express in 1963; M6 construction work was well underway by then. (Howard Leach)

SCORTON

WESTERN RAILWAY

B.M.86·7

S.P.s

Scorton Station

S.B.

S.P.s

Weir

Park Brook

Mill Race

Scorton Factory
(Disused)

B.M.89·8

Institute

Lodge

Smy.
B.M.92·7

Tk.

Wesleyan
Methodist Chapel

Springfield

F.P.

F.P.

F.P.

F.P.

Stepping
Stones

h Wood

Dg.

C.R.

Mill

S.

Mill Pond

S.

Scorton
Hall

St. Mary

Presby

School

Vicarage

St. Pete
Churc

Grave Yard

Bowling
Green

XIII. The first station opened by the L&PJR on 26th June 1840 was very short-lived, one and a half months in fact, and replaced in August of that year by another about half a mile to the north and nearer to the village of Scorton. The station was closed by the LMS on 1st May 1939 but Station Lane, that passes under the line going west from the village, survives to this day. Nothing remains of either station save for the aforementioned road. The village of Scorton is host to an annual Steam Weekend that takes place around Father's Day every June and is reputed to be the biggest such fair in the North West.

77. An undated view of the station looking south from the up platform. (Stations UK)

78. An early picture of Scorton station high on the WCML embankment. Station Lane passes under the bridge. (Mark Bartlett coll.)

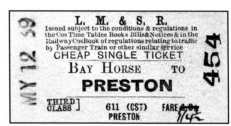

MY 12 39

L. M. & S. R.
Issued subject to the conditions & regulations in the Cos Time Tables Books Bills & Notices & in the Railway Cos Book of regulations relating to traffic by Passenger Train or other similar service
CHEAP SINGLE TICKET
BAY HORSE   TO
PRESTON
THIRD CLASS]   611 (CST)   FARE
PRESTON

454

79. On 19th April 2018 BR class 37 no. 37403 *Isle of Mull* powers through Scorton crossing over Station Lane. The Monday to Friday Carlisle to Preston and return service to Barrow were class 37 powered on Tuesdays and Thursdays and the final service was on 17th May 2018. (Mark Bartlett)

80. LMS 5MT 4-6-0 no. 45291 passes over the River Wyre just to the north of Scorton station on 26th August 1954 with the 14.15 Preston to Barrow service.
(Cumbrian Railways Association Pearsall collection ref PEG246)

BAY HORSE

Hole of Ellel

Aqueduct

F.P.

Ford

Hole of Ellel Bridge

S.P.

Subway

Bay Horse Hotel (P.H.)

Tank

Bay Horse Station

W.M.

S.P.

Cr.

Cattle Pens

Bankrigg Cottages

S.B.

B.M.77·3

S.P.

Quarry

Fox

G.P.

Tk.

F.B. · *Fn*

M.P.

Tanner's Bridge
Lancaster 6
Garstang 4⅜
G.P.
.76

P.O.

M.S.

S.&K.R.H.

Old Quarry

LONDO

S.P.

XIV. Bay Horse was another station to be named after a nearby inn. Opened by the L&PJR on 26th June 1840 and later the hamlet of Bay Horse developed around the station, shown on this 1912 map.

Bay Horse is memorable for being the site of several accidents, the first of which occurred in the early 1840s. Engine driver, Jack Smith, frustrated at having to wait on a Sunday for the level crossing gates to be opened threatened to drive through the closed gates. On a July Sunday in 1840, he carried out the threat but in the process derailed his locomotive; fortunately there were no injuries. A fatal collision did occur at the station in August 1848. An L&CR London to Glasgow express ran into the back of a L&PJR local train; coaches were smashed and derailed; several passengers were injured and unfortunately one was killed. Finally on 24th October 1861 a further incident occurred at the station, when a down mail train collided with a goods train; only the driver, fireman and one passenger were injured.

The station closed to passengers on 13th June 1960 and to goods on 18th May 1964 outlasting all other intermediate stations other than Garstang and Catterall. Visit the site of the station today and one can still see the ramp to the cattle dock, the goods shed, the subway linking the platforms, which is still in use, and the station master's house. The level crossing referred to above served Whams Lane, which was later diverted and passes under the line just north of the station leading to the crossing being removed.

In 1964, Bay Horse was host to cement trains from the Blue Circle works in Snodland in Kent - see picture 101. The cement was offloaded into two silos provided in the goods yard used for surfacing the nearby M6 motorway.

81. A northward view shows the goods yard and signal box in the distance.
(Cumbrian Railways Association Jackson collection ref JA1185)

→ 82. A 1905 shot of Bay Horse station looking south.
(Stations UK)

83. BR class 68 Bo-Bo diesel electric locomotives no. 68034 *Victorious* (nameplates not yet fitted) and no. 68018 *Vigilant* haul three nuclear flasks from Crewe to Sellafield past the site of Bay Horse on 21st February 2019. Note the former goods shed beyond the train.
(Mark Bartlett coll.)

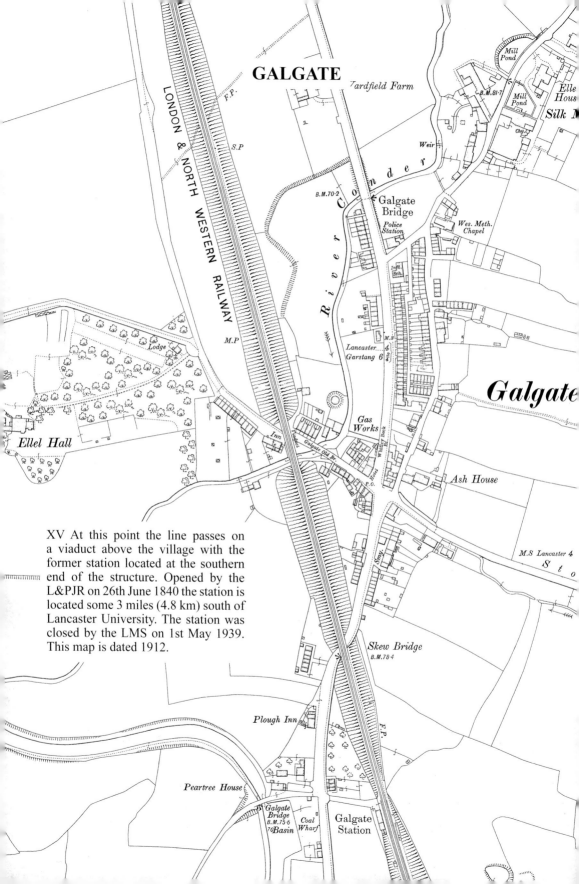

GALGATE

Yardfield Farm

LONDON & NORTH WESTERN RAILWAY

F.P.

S.P

Mill Pond

B.M.81·7

Mill Pond

Chy

Elle House

Silk M

Weir

River Conder

B.M.70·2

Galgate Bridge

Police Station

Wes. Meth. Chapel

Inft. Schl.

M.P

Lodge

M.S
4

Lancaster
Garstang 6

Galgate

Ellel Hall

Inn

Galgate Old Br.

Whitby Head Br. Road

Gas Works

Ash House

P.O.

M.S Lancaster 4

S t o

Stray

XV At this point the line passes on a viaduct above the village with the former station located at the southern end of the structure. Opened by the L&PJR on 26th June 1840 the station is located some 3 miles (4.8 km) south of Lancaster University. The station was closed by the LMS on 1st May 1939. This map is dated 1912.

Skew Bridge
B.M.78·4

Plough Inn

F.P.

Peartree House

Galgate Bridge
B.M.75·6
Basin

Coal Wharf

Galgate Station

London & North Western Ry.

Issued subject to the conditions & regulations in
the Cos Time Tables Books Bills & Notices.

BAY HORSE TO

LANCASTER (CAS.) (L&NW)

Second] 611(S) [Class

LANCASTER(C.) FARE -/7

2592

84. Galgate station looking south in 1900.
(Robert Humm coll.)

85. Looking north in around 1912 shows the station building on the down platform, which was accessed off the A6. (LOSA)

86. Freight trains cross on the Skew bridge carrying the line over the A6 trunk road, just north of the station, probably in the early 1960s.
(Cumbrian Railways Association Connop-Price collection ref MCP086)

87. An unidentified BR class 50 hauls a down service over the Galgate Viaduct on 21st August 1972. Class 50s were the mainstay of main line traction after steam and prior to electrification of the WCML north of Preston. (Tom Heavyside)

88. On 6th March 2022 ex-LMS Jubilee class 4-6-0 no. 45699 *Galatea* (masquerading as either 45562 *Alberta* or 45627 *Sierra Leone*) headed West Coast Railways' 'The Peaks Express' from Preston to Derby and return, seen here crossing the Condor viaduct. A BR class 47 from the Company was on the rear. (Will Smith)

89. On 25th July 1981 class 86/0 no. 86033 leaves Oubeck down goods loop with 6P66 07.20 (SO) Stanlow - Hardendale Quarry LPG tanks. (Peter Smith)

LANCASTER

Former L&PJR terminus

← XVI. A few miles north of Galgate marks the location of Lancaster Old Junction on this 6ins map of 1895. The point where the former L&PJR line terminated at the end of Penny Street can be seen circled and its location is to the southeast of Lancaster Castle station. The station is referred to variously as Lancaster, Lancaster Penny Street and Lancaster Greaves; the latter being the city district where it was located. By the time this map was drawn up passenger services had ceased but freight activity continued until 1967.

According to the working timetable from 13th June to 18th September 1955 and 11th June to 16th September 1956, the class E SO 5.15am freight service from Carlisle Upperby to Lancaster No. 1 arrived at 8.35am and was held over on the former L&PJR line and went forward to Bushbury at 8.50pm later in the day. This was a regular SO working that continued until the early 1960s.

90. On 22nd June 1949 Black Five 4-6-0 no. 45185 passes Lancaster Old Junction and Signal Box No. 1 with an up goods. The lines to the right of the locomotive head towards the former terminus. (Cumbrian Railways Association Pearsall collection ref PEP094)

91. A view of Lancaster Old junction on 2nd June 1968 looking south with an out of use water column on the left and No. 1 box on the right. Originally the signal box was located alongside the up line - see map opposite. The WCML from Lancaster can be seen converging from the right. (Cumbrian Railways Association Pearsall collection ref A68-12-5)

92. On 22nd June 1949 BR WD 2-8-0 no. 90331 on a
Heysham - Preston freight service approaches Lancaster
Old Junction with the loco shed in the background
adjacent to the L&PJR tracks. Note the water tank on the
roof of the shed above the tracks.
(Cumbrian Railways Association Pearsall
collection ref PEP093)

93. A view of the former L&PJR engine shed at Ripley,
Scotforth, taken on 2nd June 1968. The ancient shed was
known as 'Bridge Road' but was sometimes referred to
as the 'Dog Kennel'. (Cumbrian Railways Association
Pearsall collection ref A68-12-4)

London & North Western Ry.

Issued subject to the conditions & regulations in the Cos Time Tables Books Bills & Notices.

LANCASTER (CASTLE) TO

CARNFORTH (L.&N.W.)

(E)

THIRD CLASS] 613(S.) CARNFORTH [Parly FARE -/6½

8281

06 AP 60

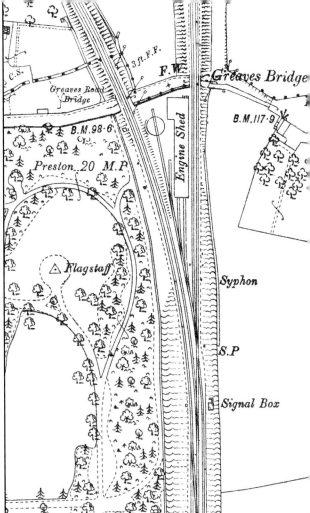

XVII. This map of 1893 shows clearly the engine shed and turntable and the signal box on the up side of the WCML. The box on the up side was installed by the L&C c1869. The box installed on the down side was an LNWR type 5 cabin that dates from June 1905. The engine shed referred to as 'Ripley' shed was originally under Preston control but later transferred to Carnforth. The shed closed on 4th February 1934 and staff and some locomotives were transferred to Lancaster Green Ayre.

94. The former goods shed looking south on 2nd June 1968.
(Cumbrian Railways Association Pearsall collection ref A68-12-7)

95. Another view of the former goods shed on the same day looking north. (Cumbrian Railways Association Pearsall collection ref A68-12-6)

96. LNWR Webb 1P Waterloo class 2-4-0 no. 5100 *Engineer Lancaster* was the third locomotive to carry that name. Though the date is unknown, it is seen facing north outside the loco shed. Note the faint outline of its original nameplate on the large splasher above the leading driving wheel. This would have carried its original name, *Roberts*. The nameplate you see was directly acquired from her predecessor, an LNWR 'Small Bloomer' class 2-2-2. (Lancaster Museum)

97. An undated photo of 16ton mineral wagons at the end of the truncated L&PJR line at Lancaster. The line closed for freight on 14th August 1967 and the tracks were taken up by 1969. (Graham Hibbert/Michael Bolton coll.)

98. On 23rd May 1964 BR 6MT Clan 4-6-2 no. 72007 *Clan MacKintosh* worked the 1Z12 RCTS 'Ribble - Lune Railtour' seen here at the site of the former L&PJR goods yard in Lancaster. (Ron Herbert)

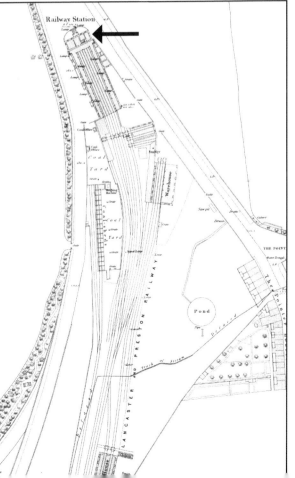

← XVIII. OS 60ins Town Plan as at 1845 showing the LP&JR tracks leading to the coal yard on the left, warehouses to the right and the terminus ahead. An arrow indicates the terminal building. Remnants of the platforms in the coal yard can be seen in the Royal Lancaster Infirmary car park off Ashton Road.

99. Taken on 25th January 2021, this impressive sandstone building, designed by Edwin Gwyther a Birmingham architect, served as Lancaster station, terminus of the L&PJR. It had a ceremonial opening on 25th June 1840 with regular passenger services commencing the next day. Following the leasing of the L&PJR by the L&CR on 1st August 1849, the station was closed to passengers, who were then obliged to use Lancaster Castle station from that date. The building also housed the offices of the L&PJR. Today the building is used by the NHS. (Roy Davies)

← *Inset: On the same day this photo of the commemorative plaque was shot. (Roy Davies)*

CITY OF LANCASTER

TERMINUS OF THE
LANCASTER & PRESTON
JUNCTION RAILWAY
AND LANCASTER'S
FIRST STATION
1840 - 46

HERITAGE BUILDING

South of Lancaster station and the goods yard

100. BR WD class 2-8-0 no. 90640 hauls a Heysham-Lostock goods service past the sidings south of Lancaster Castle station on 18th May 1951. The actual castle can be seen in the background high above the station. (Cumbrian Railways Association Pearsall collection ref PEQ059)

101. Black 5 4-6-0 no. 44874 is with Ivatt 2-6-2T no. 41215 banking as it departs from Lancaster Castle, hauling the 5M27 22.50 Snodland to Bay Horse block train of Presflo cement wagons and brake van on 1st July 1964. Due to constraints in the layout at Bay Horse, the loaded train needed to run on the down line to Lancaster; reverse and return to Bay Horse on the up line for unloading. The empties returned to Kent as 4O27 17.50 Bay Horse to Snodland. (Ron Herbert)

Tennis Ground

S.Ps

Vicarage

Grave Yard

St. Mary's Church
(Vicarage)
B.M.133·7

B.M.107·6

S.D.
Site of
ROMAN STATION

Almshouses

ST. MARYS GATE

B.M.89·9

Judges' Lodge.

B.M.69·1

HILL SIDE

LONG MARSH LANE

CASTLE PARADE

D.F.

SHIRE HALL

LANCASTER
CASTLE
(His Majesty's Prison)

Adrian's Tower
B.M.116·8

ST. MARYS PARADE

Gateway
Tower

CASTLE HILL

B.M.55·8

CASTLE

PARK

Turn.

B.M.107·2

B.M. 75·9

Storey
Institute

L.B.

Station Road

County Hotel

Castle Station

F.B.

S.D.

B.M.56·4

B.M. 83·4

Burial Ground

School

Friends'
Meeting House

MEETING HOUSE LANE

B.M.84·0

FENTON STREET

Friends'
Hall

KELSEY STREET

LINCOLN ROAD

S.P.

S.P.

S.B.

Cattle Pens

WHEATFIELD

DALLAS ROAD

Goods Shed

Cranes

STREET

Crane

SIBSEY STREET

INGATE-SAUL ROAD

BLADES STREET

S.P.

← XIX. This 1913 map shows the remodelled Lancaster Castle, as well as the goods yard and sidings south of the station. The main building on the western side was built by William Tite in 1846 in Tudor Revival style. The original plan was to route the line following the Lancaster Canal across the River Lune from Ladies Walk to Skerton. This was abandoned in favour of the current and cheaper option crossing the Lune via the Carlisle Bridge but required a steep incline of 1 in 98 towards Lancaster Old Junction - see Map XVI.

During the years 1900 to 1906, the station was subject to substantial remodelling that included: additional station buildings; a new entrance and offices on the eastern side; additional platforms and through lines. Platforms 5 and 6 were added on the eastern side; the latter to accommodate Midland Railway Morecambe 'electrics' and accordingly platform 6 was electrified in 1908 but platform 5 not until the 1950s. With the closure of the Morecambe and Heysham line to passengers in January 1966, the track alongside platform 6 was later removed together with the associated OLE. On 5th May 1969 the station was renamed 'Lancaster'.

In 1973 there was further track rationalisation prior to WCML electrification and signalling came under the control of the Preston power box. Passenger services under the WCML wires commenced on 7th May 1974.

The Covid pandemic aside, Lancaster station is host to over two million passengers per year boosted no doubt by Lancaster University and can boast of being fully accessible to disabled passengers.

Work continues to improve the station and on 7th April 2022 the Tite & Locke pub was opened in previously unused offices on platform 3, near platforms 1 and 2.

102. D228 *Samaria* is hauling a northbound oil tank freight past Lancaster No. 3 box and is taking the down through line on 21st August 1972. (Tom Heavyside)

The station

103. An external shot of the main station building on the western side of the complex taken on 14th July 1952. (Robert Humm coll.)

104. An undated view looking north prior to the major rebuild between 1898 and 1902. The stone bridge in the background carries Meeting House Lane over the railway; it was later replaced by a girder bridge. (LOSA)

105. A pre-grouping view c1910 looks north towards Carlisle from platform 3 after reconstruction in 1902. OLE for the Morecambe electrics, introduced in 1908, can be seen north of platform 4. (LOSA)

Inset: Seen on a door frame on platform 3 at Castle station was writing that revealed the Office of the Lancaster and Preston Junction railway. (Ron Herbert)

106. English Electric GT3 4-6-0 passes through Lancaster Castle on the up main line working a test train on 18th October 1961. GT3, meaning Gas Turbine number 3 following Nos. 1 (18000) and 2 (18100), was built at Vulcan Foundry, Newton le Willows in 1961. There were design issues, matching the convenience of new double-ended diesel locomotives among others, and funding was not forthcoming. GT3 was stored at the Vulcan foundry in late 1962 and scrapped in 1966. (Ron Herbert)

107. Morecambe electric unit no. M29023M stands in platform 6 ready to depart for Heysham via Lancaster Green Ayre on 13th May 1963. (*ColourRail.com*/J. Tolson)

108. On 1st April 1967 BR Standard 4-6-2 Britannia class no. 70028 *Royal Star* is standing in platform 5 alongside classmate no. 70010 *Owen Glendower* in platform 6. Both locomotives were working on Carlisle to Crewe mail trains and coincidentally both were withdrawn in September of that year. By then no. 70010 was running without nameplates, although its hand-painted name could be seen on the smoke deflectors. (Michael Ellis)

109. BR Sulzer type 2 class 24 diesel no. 24 027 stands in platform 5 in April 1975 acting as the trip loco that day. It bore the usual headcode '0T49' making any local movements between Lancaster, Morecambe, Heysham and Carnforth. A class 24 on this duty was quite unusual and it is likely it found its way up from Crewe. (Jonathan Dixon)

110. Three class 40s stand in platform 5 on 2nd June 1976 ready to drag electric trains south due to overhead power lines being vandalised at Preston. (Jonathan Dixon)

111. On 29th May 1982 BR class 40 no. 40126 (originally D326) arrives in platform 3 on the 09.15 Liverpool - Barrow service. (Tom Heavyside)

➜ 112. BR class 87 Bo-Bo no. 87001 *Royal Scot* (originally *Stephenson* but that was transferred to 87101) is seen at platform 3 with the 09.13 Birmingham New Street - Edinburgh service on 20th June 1992. The locomotive would have recently been repainted into Intercity Swallow livery from its previous Intercity Executive livery. This locomotive has been preserved and can be seen at the National Railway Museum. (Tom Heavyside)

↓ 113. First TransPennine Express class 185 DMU no. 185147 arriving from Windermere buffers up to DMU no. 185102 from Barrow-in-Furness in platform 5 before going forward together as the 15.15 to Manchester Airport on 23rd July 2008. (Mark Bartlett)

114. London Midland class 350 EMU no. 350372 is with a northbound TransPennine service on 13th August 2014. This was one of two sets hired by TPE to strengthen its services during the Commonwealth Games that year. (Mark Bartlett)

115. BR class 397 no. 397008 arrives at platform 4 on 17th September 2020 with a Manchester Airport service. The CAF Civity arrangement is also utilised on the TransPennine class 397 EMUs under the classification of Nova 2 (the Nova 1 being class 802 BMU sets and locomotive-hauled CAF-built Mark 5A coaches designated Nova 3). (*ColourRail.com*/Paul Chancellor)

116. BR class 325s operated by DB Cargo with no. 325008 *Peter Howarth CBE* brings up the rear at platform 3 on the Willesden - Shieldmuir Royal Mail service with the balancing southbound service in platform 4 opposite on 28th October 2021. The units were stopped unusually at Lancaster for a crew change due to disruptions to all services caused by atrocious weather conditions to the north and across the border on the 27th and 28th October. (Alan Smith)

117. BR class 60/0 no. 66177, still in EWS livery, heads the 14.16 Seaforth (Merseyside) to Mossend (North Lanarkshire) service crossing a southbound Manchester Airport service operated by TransPennine Express class 397 EMU no. 397007 on 5th May 2022. (Roy Davies)

118. An Edinburgh to Euston via Birmingham service, formed of two unidentified Super Voyagers, stands in Lancaster's platform 3 on 1st June 2022. Note the Avanti West Coast livery. (Mark Bartlett)

119. An Avanti Pendolino class 390/1 set no. 390156 pulls into platform 4 on 1st June 2022 with a Glasgow - Euston Service. This unit was one of the last four ordered by then Virgin Trains between 2010 and 2012. Set no. 390156 was formerly named *Stockport 170* when delivered in 2013 and was renamed *Pride and Prosperity* on 9th December 2019 to celebrate the launch of Avanti West Coast operations on the West Coast Partnership franchise. (Mark Bartlett)

120. Just south of Lancaster station, West Coast Railways' SR Merchant Navy class 4-6-2 no. 35018 *British India Line* storms under the A588 Ashton Road on 8th June 2021 heading the Pendle Dalesman excursion while attacking the 1 in 98 gradient as it rounds the curve towards the site of Lancaster Old Junction - see map XVI. The rail tour was from Lancaster to Carlisle and returned via Blackburn and Hellifield. (Will Smith)

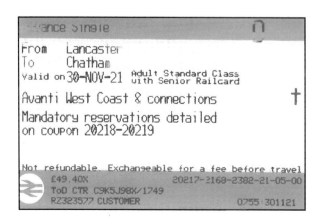

Further views of Lancaster can be seen in *Wennington to Morecambe and Heysham* **and forthcoming album,** *Lancaster to Oxenholme (including the LNWR branches to Morecambe and Windermere).*

EVOLVING THE ULTIMATE RAIL ENCYCLOPEDIA

Vic Mitchell and Keith Smith

INTERNATIONAL

126a Camelsdale Road, GU27 3RJ. Tel:01730 813169

A-978 0 906520	B- 978 1 873793	C- 978 1 901706	D-978 1 904474
E - 978 1 906008	F - 978 1 908174	G - 978 1 910356	